Horses

CONTENTS

Horses and their relatives	4
Grazing animals	6
Running for life	8
Social life	11
Mothers and young	12
Zebras	14
The wild asses and half-asses	16
True wild horses	18
Domesticated horses	20
Domestic asses	22
Heavy horses	24
Arabs and Thoroughbreds	26
Ponies	28
Horses today	30
Glossary	32
Index	32

© Aladdin Books Ltd 1986

Designed and produced by
Aladdin Books Ltd
70 Old Compton Street
London W1

First published in the
United States in 1987 by
Gloucester Press
387 Park Avenue South
New York NY 10016

Printed in Belgium

ISBN 0-531-17039-X

Library of Congress Catalog
Card Number 86-82690

Certain illustrations have previously appeared in the "Closer Look"
series published by Gloucester Press.

The consultant on this book, JL Cloudsley-Thompson,
is Professor of Zoology, Birkbeck College,
University of London, UK.

A CLOSER LOOK AT

Horses

JOYCE POPE

Illustrated by
PETER BARRETT

Consultant
J. L. CLOUDSLEY-THOMPSON

Gloucester Press
New York · Toronto · 1987

Horses and their relatives

There is a wide range of different types and breeds of horses, from the massive Shire horse to the tiny Shetland pony. There are great differences in size, build, color and even behavior. This great range is largely the result of people cross-breeding horses.

Horses and people have lived and worked together since between 3,000 BC and 2,000 BC. People learned centuries ago that they could breed horses to be strong, fast or small, depending on what work they required of them, by carefully matching a foal's parents.

Grouping horses

Horses are members of the equid animal family. The name equid comes from the Latin word *equus*, meaning "horse." The equids are part of a larger group of animals known as the "odd-toed hoofed" animals.

The rhinoceros and tapir are the closest relatives of the horses. They are all odd-toed hoofed animals. They have this strange name because they all walk on their toes, putting most of their weight on the middle toe. Today, however, all members of the horse or equid family have only one toe, which is protected by a large toenail, or hoof. Their immediate ancestors had three toes.

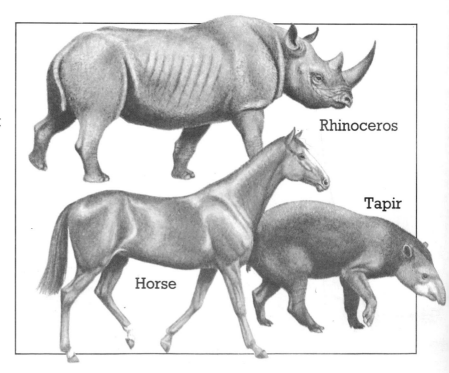

Rhinoceros

Tapir

Horse

The equid family

The equid family includes the Mongolian wild horse, which is sometimes called Przewalski's horse. This is the ancestor of all domestic breeds of horses. Donkeys and the wild asses of north Africa are also members of this family, as are the several kinds of "hemiones" or half-asses of the dry plains of Asia. Most wild horses have some stripes on their bodies. Zebras are striped all over.

It is possible for these animals to interbreed. A cross between a horse and a donkey is called a mule; a cross between a horse and zebra is called a zebroid.

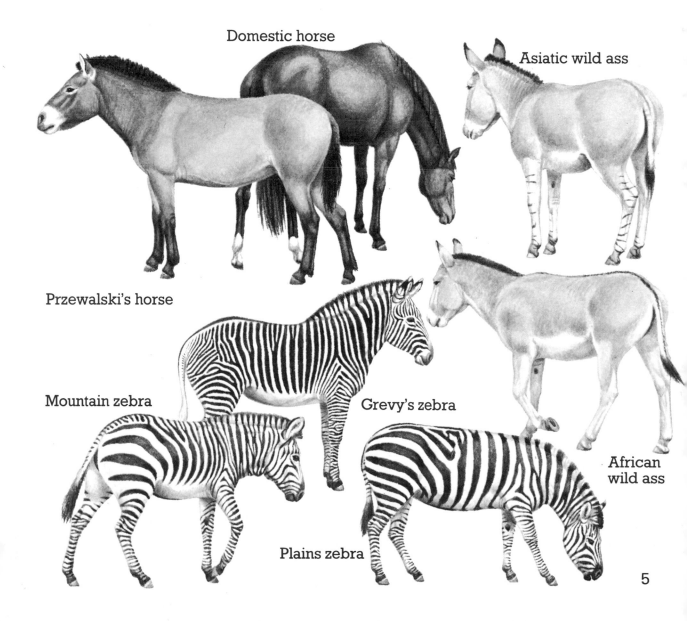

Domestic horse

Asiatic wild ass

Przewalski's horse

Mountain zebra

Grevy's zebra

African wild ass

Plains zebra

Grazing animals

All members of the horse family are basically grass-eating or grazing animals. All wild horses live on dry plains where few plants except grasses will grow. In order to have enough food, wild horses may move from one pasture area to another throughout the year.

Asses and half-asses can go without drinking for long periods, but the other species must always be able to get to water every day.

All members of the horse family have long heads and necks. Because of this they are easily able to reach the ground with their mouths, and feed even when the pasture is very short. They prefer fresh, growing grass a few inches high.

While a horse has its head down feeding, it is still able to keep a sharp look out for human beings and the large flesh-eaters which are its main enemies. It is able to do this because its eyes are placed far back on the sides of its head, so it can see behind as well as to the sides and the front.

Horses' teeth

Grasses are very tough plants so horses need large, strong teeth. In the front of their mouths they have six biting teeth in each jaw and these crop the blades of grass. The back teeth are like grinding millstones. Grasses are so harsh that these teeth get worn down, but a horse's teeth continue to grow throughout its life.

Selecting food

There are many kinds of grasses. Each type probably has its own special taste because as horses graze they select what they want to eat from among all the plants in the pasture. They can do this because their nostrils are near the ground so they can smell anything especially nice or unpleasant. Their lips, particularly their upper lips, are very flexible so they can pick and choose easily. Domesticated horses may be fed on more nutritious food such as oats to give them more energy for work.

Running for life

Horses' main defenses against their enemies lie in their alertness and their ability to run away from danger. Like a racing car, they can accelerate within seconds from a standing start to a gallop which may be as fast as 60km (37 miles) per hour. At such a speed they soon tire, but even at a slightly slower pace, which they are able to keep going for hours, horses still move faster than most other animals can run.

Gaits of a horse

Horses move their legs differently at different speeds. These changes in the pattern of movement are called the gaits of the horse. At a walk, each leg is moved in turn, and the animal is always supported by two feet on the ground. At a trot, one fore and one hindleg on each side are moved forward together at a greater speed than at the walk. At the highest speeds, called the canter and the gallop, the two fore and two hindlegs are used in a bounding motion and there is a moment in each stride when no foot is touching the ground.

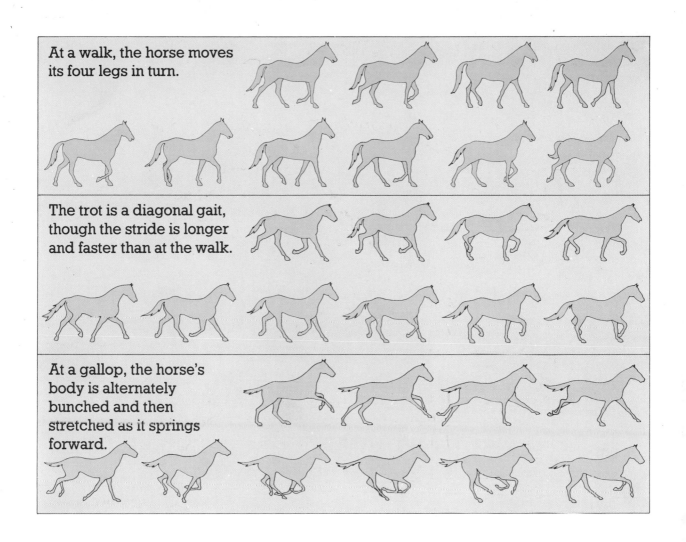

At a walk, the horse moves its four legs in turn.

The trot is a diagonal gait, though the stride is longer and faster than at the walk.

At a gallop, the horse's body is alternately bunched and then stretched as it springs forward.

Zebras can keep up a steady canter for many miles.

9

Most of the time horses are peaceable, but fierce-looking battles may take place between stallions.

Social life

All members of the horse family are social animals and they need the company of their own kind. Domestic horses and ponies usually appear unhappy if they are kept alone.

Wild horses live in family groups, consisting of a dominant male or stallion, with several females or mares and their offspring. Even a very large herd of horses is made up of these separate families, each consisting of about a dozen animals.

Advantages of the herd

The family is usually led on its wanderings by the oldest mare. Because each animal is constantly alert, there is a good chance that any danger will be seen while it is still a long way off. If any member of the herd is sick or injured, the rest of the herd will help to protect it and the stallion in particular will defend his mares and foals against enemies. Young mares will leave the family and join another group when they grow up. Males remain for longer, but eventually leave to join a bachelor group. They do not take over families of their own until they are about six years old.

Mothers and young

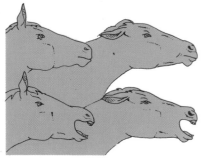

Horses communicate with each other in many ways, using scent, body language and facial expressions. Ears may be laid back in fear or anger or pricked forward in curiosity or friendship.

Within a family group, horses have their own special friends. These may be seen standing together peaceably, resting their heads on each others' backs, or grooming by nibbling at each others' skin.

The stallion is the father of all the foals in his group. They may be born at any time of the year, but generally arrive when there is plenty of good food available, either in the springtime or, in tropical areas, in the rainy season. It is rare for a mare to produce twins, for the foals are very large. They are able to stand within about fifteen minutes of being born, ready to run if the herd is in danger. They stay very close to their mothers for several days.

The foal grows up

When it is a few days old, a foal begins to explore away from its mother's side. It will get to know the other members of the family, especially the other babies in the group. It plays racing games with them, developing its strength and speed. But it will always return to its own mother, because she is the only one who will feed it.

A foal's first year

A foal starts to nibble grass well before it is weaned but it is given milk by its mother for at least the first eight months of its life and in some cases for longer. The mare is ready to mate again soon after the birth of her foal and, where food is good, wild horses and zebras usually produce one foal each year.

Zebras

There are three different species of zebras, all found in Africa. Best known is the Plains zebra, which lives in large herds in east and southern Africa. Much rarer is the Mountain zebra, which is found in a few places in the south and southeast, and Grevy's zebra which lives in Ethiopia and northern Kenya. No two zebras have exactly the same pattern of stripes. It is certain that the Plains and Mountain zebras are able to recognize their families and friends because of this.

Different lifestyles

Plains zebras and Mountain zebras spend much of their lives on the move, seeking fresh pasture, so they do not have a fixed home region or territory. In spite of this, they lead highly organized lives, in which each member of a family group knows its place. Grevy's zebras do not form such stable family units. Some of the males hold large territories, which they will defend against others.

The stripes of the Plains zebras differ from one region of Africa to another. Mountain zebras differ from Plains zebras in having a series of crossways stripes, called a gridiron pattern, across the lower back and base of the tail. Mountain males have a fold of skin or dewlap on the lower side of the neck.

The wild asses and half-asses

A few long-eared, gray members of the horse family survive in remote, dry, rocky areas of north Africa. These are the wild asses – tough, hardy and surefooted but almost certainly doomed to extinction as more of their homelands are taken by man and they are destroyed unmercifully. A now extinct race of these creatures probably gave rise to the domestic donkey.

Asiatic asses

The hemiones, sometimes called the half-asses, live on the semidesert plains of Asia. There are several kinds of these golden colored animals. All are now very rare in the wild, though some survive in zoos or reserves.

In the desert, hemiones sometimes go without drinking, obtaining the moisture that they need from succulent plants. They can run at high speed over very rough ground.

The kiang from the high plateau of Tibet is the most horselike of the half-asses. It lives in tightly organized herds, but without much of the contact and mutual grooming found in the true horses.

North African wild asses are larger and sleeker than the domestic donkey.

African wild ass

Mule

Donkey

True wild horses

During prehistoric times wild horses lived on the cold plains of Europe and Asia. They were an important source of food for Stone Age man, who often painted pictures of them on the walls of caves.

Przewalski's horses

Today the great herds of these animals no longer exist. Their numbers dwindled as the climate became warmer and their habitat changed. In Europe the remainder were hunted to extinction. In Asia their last stronghold was a mountainous area on the border of China and Mongolia where they were discovered during the last century by an explorer called Colonel Przewalski. Even these may now be extinct, for they have not been seen in the wild recently. Some survive in zoos and wildlife parks.

Now extinct, the tarpan was a small, gray colored horse, with a stripe down its back. It had a falling mane and long tail like domestic horses, rather than the upright mane and shorter, stiffer tail of the Asiatic wild horses.

The tarpan

The tarpan was a type of wild horse that lived in Europe and western Asia. Some people think that it was the tarpan, rather than Przewalski's horse, which was first tamed and bred by man. Herds of wild tarpans used to raid farmers' crops, so they were totally destroyed early in the last century.

Because it is known what the tarpan was like, it has been possible to breed small horses, very similar to it in appearance. Now many of these "back-bred" tarpans are to be seen in zoos and reserves.

North Franklin ERC

Domesticated horses

Some people think that Old Stone Age men in Europe began the process of taming wild horses. However, horses were probably not domesticated until very much later than this – perhaps not until about 4,000 years ago.

At first, they were used mainly for food. Later, in Mesopotamia and Egypt, it was discovered that they could pull lightweight chariots, though heavy loads were still drawn by oxen. Horses were not ridden until still later. For many centuries people rode bareback, until saddles were invented.

The importance of horses

As the mounts of warriors and the carriers of burdens, horses have had a greater effect on human history than any other animal. In early times they enabled people to travel to distant places and to conquer new lands.

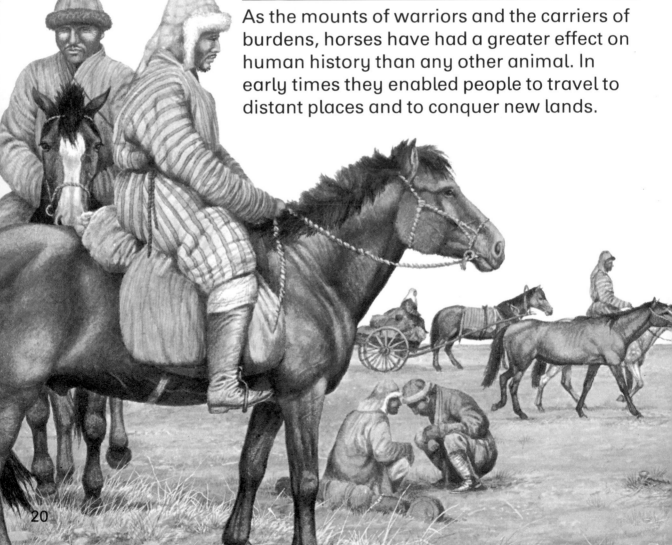

Nomads and their horses

In central Asia much of the land is now taken over by agriculture. But in some areas there are still wandering peoples or nomads who live in the traditional way, following their herds from place to place in search of water and grazing. They are totally dependent on their horses, which are small, very hardy animals, capable of standing the great heat of the summers and extreme cold of the winter months. The nomads use them not only for transportation, but also get meat, hides for leather, and even milk from them.

Today, horses have been replaced by other forms of transportation over much of the world. But they are still ridden by people who herd cattle or sheep over large areas where there are few roads. In the United States and Australia, horses are still used in this way.

Life has changed little over the ages for the horse-riding nomads of central Asia.

Domestic asses

Although zebras and hemiones have sometimes been tamed, they have never been completely domesticated. Apart from the true horses, the only member of the horse family to become a slave of human beings is the donkey. This animal is the descendant of a form of the north African wild ass which was tamed in the Middle East by men of the New Stone Age.

Dry country animals

Donkeys are usually found in hot or dry countries, carrying or pulling heavy loads, for they can survive on poor food in harsh, dry conditions. They are generally smaller than the true wild asses and are sometimes crossed with horses to produce mules. These are bigger than donkeys and tougher and more surefooted than either of their parents.

Perhaps because of their docility, donkeys are often mistreated and overloaded.

Heavy horses

In the early days of domestication, horses were small. As time went on, some people mated their largest stallions and mares together and gradually breeds of bigger and stronger animals were produced.

This was particularly important in the Middle Ages when a knight in full armor needed a very powerful horse to carry him. These war horses were also armored, adding greatly to the weight which they had to support.

Most breeds of heavy horse seen today were developed to work on farms.

Clydesdale

Suffolk Punch

Percheron

Ardennes

Dutch Draft

Strong as they were, the war horses of the Middle Ages were slow and awkward. They were finally made useless in battle by the invention of guns.

Farm horses

Such huge horses were capable of carrying heavy loads. From them, modern breeds for farm work and drawing carts have been developed.

For centuries, in many parts of the world, horses took over from oxen as the main draft animals on farms. Today they have been replaced by tractors almost everywhere. One reason for this is that a farm using horses needed about a third of its land to grow food for them – the horses had to eat, whether or not they were working.

Nowadays it is acknowledged that horses do less damage to the soil than heavy tractors. Consequently a few farmers are using horses again for part of their work and people are having to relearn the skills of managing horses.

Plowing with a team of horses took skill. One acre, about the size of a football field, was the area that a man and his horses were expected to be able to plow in one day.

Arabs and Thoroughbreds

The Arab horses are small and elegant but nevertheless very tough. They have been molded by generations of harsh desert life, in which the survival of their owners has often depended on the speed and endurance of these hardy horses.

Thoroughbreds

In early days, Arab horses were greatly prized on the rare occasions that they came to Europe. In the late 17th century, three stallions were brought to Britain and mated with mares of northern breeds. Their offspring had the sleekness and beauty of the Arabs, but were larger and faster. They gave rise to the Thoroughbreds which today are the mainstay of horse racing.

Arabs have been crossed with some pony breeds, particularly the New Forest and the Welsh ponies in Britain. This has produced new lines of stronger, finer ponies.

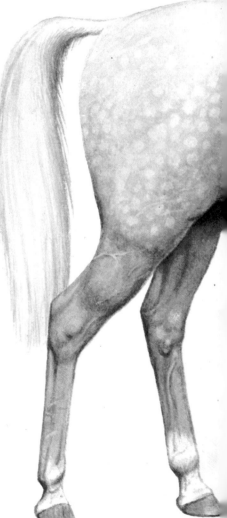

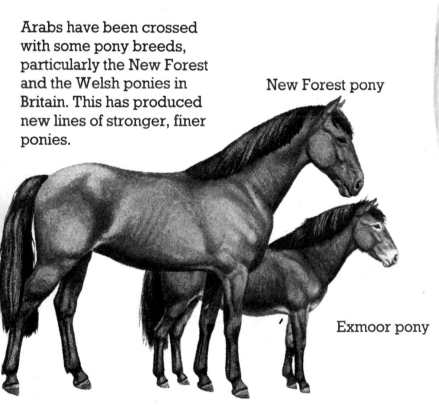

New Forest pony

Exmoor pony

English Thoroughbreds

All English Thoroughbreds alive today can be traced back to the three Arab ancestors. Crosses are still made between Arabs and other breeds. This is done in an effort to continue to produce types of horse which will suit certain purposes: fast, light animals for racing; handsome, sturdy horses for hunting and jumping.

Arab horses are small and fine skinned with high-set tails and concave or "dished" faces. They may be almost any color, but are most often chestnut or gray.

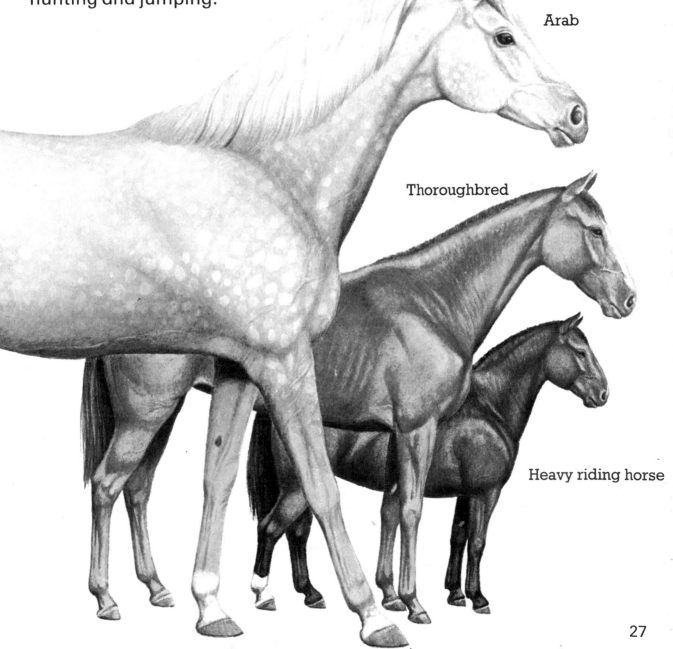

Arab

Thoroughbred

Heavy riding horse

Ponies

Over the centuries, in many parts of the world, horses escaped from captivity, or were set free in remote places. Sometimes the weather conditions were harsh and only poor food was available. Therefore the horses which survived were the small, resourceful and tough individuals, who eventually formed a number of separate breeds. These horses, rarely over 142cm (56in) at the shoulder, are known as ponies.

In the past, ponies were used as riding or pack animals, carrying loads in rough country where their hardiness and surefootedness made them more useful than larger breeds. Today, because of their small size, they are often ridden by children. Much training is needed to develop a trusting partnership between the pony and child.

Ponies kept sheltered and fed on rich food tend to increase in size, but lose some of their toughness.

Exmoor

Shetland

Timor

Norway

Camargue

Haflinger

Iceland

Exmoor ponies are said to be similar to the first horses used in Britain. Shetlands are the smallest and the hardiest of the pony breeds. Norway, Iceland and Haflinger ponies are all very strong. The Timor is nearly as small as the Shetland and is unusual in that the breed began on a tropical island.

Horses today

There are about 65 million horses in the world today, and about 200 different breeds. By carefully matching stallions and mares with special characteristics and from different areas, new types of horses can be bred.

For example, the Andalusian is a mixture of Spanish and Arab horses – strong, fast and surefooted. Mixed with the American "wild" horse, the mustang, the Andalusian has given its strength and good looks to the Quarter horse.

Some of today's 200 different types and breeds of horses have been bred for work, like England's Cleveland Bay, the United States' Morgan, Australia's Waler and Germany's Trakehner. Others, like Russia's Orlov Trotter, have been bred for sport.

Horses and sport

Nowadays, working horses are dying out, but the numbers of horses and ponies used for riding is increasing. Show-jumping and horse racing are well-known sports. Less common are competitions with horse-drawn vehicles. In the United States "Trotters" are specially bred to draw light carts.

Anglo-Arab   Orlov Trotter   Trakehner

Morgan   Waler   Quarter horse

At a horse show there are classes for all sorts of riders and their horses. Jumping and showing classes are the most serious, but there are often competitions for mounted games and even events where costumes are worn.

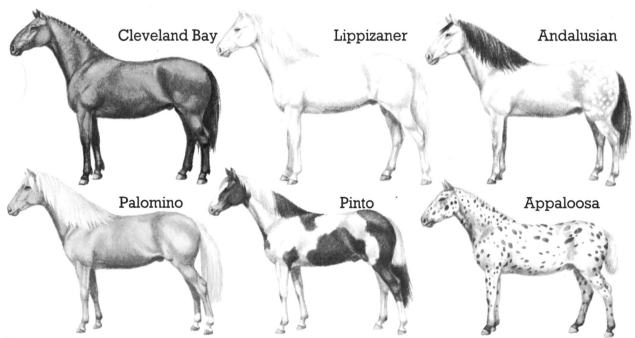

Cleveland Bay

Lippizaner

Andalusian

Palomino

Pinto

Appaloosa

Glossary

Back-breeding   Mating animals with special characteristics to produce a replica of a now-extinct species.

Dewlap   A loose flap of skin under the neck.

Domestication   The taming of a wild animal.

Equestrian   To do with the horse; from the Latin word *equus*, meaning "horse."

Equid   The animal family to which horses, zebras and asses all belong.

Foal   A young horse.

Hemione   Another name for the half-asses that live on the high Asian plains.

Kiang   A type of wild ass found in Tibet.

Mare   A female horse.

Mesopotamia   The old name for the area now called Iraq.

Stallion   A male horse.

Tapir   An odd-toed hoofed animal, found in South America and Asia.

Tarpan   An extinct wild horse, once found all over Europe.

Index

A   Arabs 26, 27, 30
asses 5, 6, 16-17

B   breeding 4, 5, 25, 26-7, 30

C   communication 12

D   domestic horses 5, 7, 11, 20-1, 24-7
donkeys 5, 16, 17, 22, 23

E   equid family 4, 5
eyes 6

F   family life 11, 12, 14

farm horses 25
foals 12, 13, 32

G   gait 8-9
grazing 6, 7

H   heavy horses 4, 24-5, 30
"hemiones" 5, 16, 22, 32

M   mares 12, 13, 24, 26, 30, 32
mules 5, 23

P   ponies 4, 26, 28-9
Przewalski's horse 5, 18, 19

S   smell 7
speed 8
stallions 10, 11, 12, 22, 26, 30, 32

T   tapir 4, 32
tarpan 18, 19, 32
teeth 7
Thoroughbreds 26, 27

W   wild horses 5, 6, 18-19

Z   zebra 5, 9, 13, 14-15, 22
zoos 18, 19

32